Horses and Foals

Fern G. Brown

HORSES
AND
FOALS

FRANKLIN WATTS 1986 A FIRST BOOK
NEW YORK LONDON TORONTO SYDNEY

Photographs courtesy of: Carol Robertson: pp. 14,15;
International Arabian Horse Association: p. 18;
the author: pp. 25, 28, 37, 40, 60, 63, 64, 70;
Percheron Horse Association of America: p. 33;
Welsh Pony Society of America, p. 47 (top);
American Connemara Pony Society: p. 47 (bottom).

Library of Congress Cataloging in Publication Data

Brown, Fern G.
Horses and foals.

(A First book)
Includes index.
Summary: An introduction, for beginning riders, to the
physical characteristics of horses and foals, their care
and training, and the history of the different breeds.
1. Horses—Juvenile literature.   2. Horse breeds—
Juvenile literature.   [1. Horses.   2. Horse breeds]
I. Title.
SF302.B76   1986   636.1   85-22634
ISBN 0-531-10118-5

Contents

Acknowledgments

The author and editor wish to express
their appreciation to the following
who have been of great assistance in
the preparation of this book:

The Illinois Equine Hospital and Clinic, Naperville, Illinois; Florence Riley, Sugarbrick American Saddle Horse Farm, Lake Zurich, Illinois; Tom Mick, retired judge, American Quarter Horse Association, Appaloosa Horse Club and Paint Horse Associations; Charles Hume of the Scientific Animal Farm, Tempel Farms, Wadsworth, Illinois; Jack McArdle; Ray Margolies; Hal M. Brown; Leonard J. Brown; Stacey L. Brown; Allison I. Brown; Cristi L. Barnett; Blaine P. Barnett; Louise Vallelonga; Beryl Boettcher; Mike Grippo; and Carol Robertson.

This book is for
Allison I. Brown,
Cristi L. Barnett, and
Stacey L. Brown—
they're horse lovers, too!

1

Especially
for
Horse Lovers

I'm a horse lover. My Appaloosa gelding, Woody Dip, is an affectionate, gentle animal, graceful when in motion—a delightful companion. The first time I looked into Woody's warm, dark eyes and stroked his shiny coat, I was hooked!

Feed my horse an apple and you've made a friend. But it's not just my horse who is a friend to humans. Horses have been our friends since ancient times when people first discovered they could be tamed and put to work.

Horses made life a whole lot easier for our ancestors. Horses carried men on their backs to hunt for food, dragged logs to clear forests for homes, pulled farmers' plows, and brought mail pouches by pony express. The only way American pioneers could have traveled overland to the West was by horse-drawn covered wagons and stagecoaches. Horses were even used to fight wars.

People depended on their faithful horses for thousands of years. Then came the invention of the automobile and everything changed. Horses were no longer needed for travel. Farmers and loggers gradually replaced their beasts of burden with tractors and heavy machinery, and soldiers used tanks to fight wars. Some people thought that horses had outlived their usefulness and would soon become extinct.

But horses haven't become extinct. Today they are more popular than ever. Many of us value them for their speed and beauty. A horse is still the best way to travel a mountain trail. Cowboys often round up cattle on horseback. Riders enjoy a canter down a wooded path for the fresh air, exercise, and beauties of nature that surround them. There are many horsepeople who hunt and jump and drive light harness, and those who exhibit at shows.

Some people enjoy breeding, raising, and training horses. Others like to see a fast horse race or an exciting polo match. Without horses, a parade, circus, or rodeo would be mighty dull. Think of the horses that work in movies and in television commercials. And what is more heartwarming than the satisfied smile on a handicapped person's face when astride a gentle, sturdy four-legged mount? There is no doubt that horses still give us a great deal of pleasure. They are and will continue to be an important part of our lives in the future.

2

Origin
and
History

More than fifty million years ago, the ancestor of our modern horse roamed the earth. Scientists came to that conclusion when they studied fossils of prehistoric animals. Bones were dug up in what is now Wyoming and New Mexico. So we know that the early horses lived right here in America.

THE FIRST HORSE

We're not sure if there were others who came before, but the first horse was named *Eohippus* (Dawn Horse), a combination of *Eo*, the Greek word for "dawn," or "beginning," and *hippus*, which means horse.

Scientists tell us that the Dawn Horse was about the size of a fox, with a thick neck, small ears, and slender legs. There were four toes on each front foot and three toes on each hind foot. Each toe ended in a tiny hoof.

Eohippus lived about sixty million years ago in the swamps and tropical forests and ate the leaves of shrubs and herbs. Always under attack by vicious animals, the Dawn Horse had no horns, claws, or sharp teeth with which to defend itself. So, in order to survive, it had to run from its enemies.

About twenty million years went by and gradually the Dawn Horse grew to about the size of a collie dog. It was called *Mesohippus*, or "middle horse." It had longer legs and only three toes on its front feet.

After a few million years, there were more changes in the little horse. Now it had grown as tall as a Shetland pony; it still had three toes on each foot, but the middle toe bore most of the animal's weight when running. This horse lived in less dense forests and prairies and it grazed on grass. Scientists named it *Merychippus*, which means a "grass-eating" horse.

Another ten million years went by and a horse that was called *Pliohippus* evolved. It was as big as a donkey and the hair on the top of its neck had become a stiff mane. It had a wider range of vision and better teeth for grazing. Another big change was its feet. The middle toe had grown harder and wider and the outside toes had gradually receded up the leg to become the splint bones of horses today.

After *Pliohippus* came *Equus*, the forerunner of the modern horse. *Equus* means "true horse." This horse was stronger and bigger than *Pliohippus*. It had long legs and its middle toe had become a hoof.

In about fifty million years *Eohippus*, the Dawn Horse, had gradually changed from a small animal the size of a fox into *Equus*, a big, strong, hooved animal. All horses today are descendants of *Equus* and belong to the family Equidae, the genus *Equus*, and the species *caballus*.

Equus ran free for millions of years. It lived in small herds that roamed the Rocky Mountain region of the United States. Some herds existed in China and Mongolia, others in Europe. The herds that roamed southwest into Asia Minor, North Africa, and the northern shores of the Mediterranean Sea produced the Arabian and the Barb horse, ancestors of almost all our modern breeds.

But about ten thousand years ago, something mysterious happened and nobody really knows why. All the horses disappeared from North America. A change in climate was probably responsible for the horse leaving.

Almost two million years ago, during a time known as the Ice Age, part of the earth became a frozen wasteland. In search of food, horses may have migrated over a land bridge that then connected Alaska to Russia. When they left, *Equus* became extinct in the Americas.

But *Equus* thrived in Europe, Asia, and Africa, and somewhere along the years, it was met by humans. At first, people hunted the horse for food and clothing. In time, it was discovered that the horse could be used for transportation and as a pack animal. We don't know when this first happened, but drawings of horses on cave walls, and various art objects, depict people and horses working together at all types of jobs.

THE HORSE GOES TO WAR

We think of horses today in connection with work or sport. But for many centuries horses were particularly important in war. In early Mesopotamian drawings most horses were pictured pulling war chariots. The use of heavy war chariots massed together made a succession of Near Eastern nations almost undefeatable until about 330 B.C. when Alexander the Great of Macedonia changed war tactics.

Mounted on light, fast horses, Alexander's bowmen easily outfought the big, clumsy chariots. Because of his cavalry, Alexander won many battles and conquered the then-civilized world.

During the European Middle Ages, the knights began to dress themselves and their war horses in more and heavier armor. So they had to breed their horses to be bigger and stronger. One important new type of horse was the Great Horse. These strong beasts were used as war mounts as well as in tournaments, in which rival knights rode at each other with lances.

During the Crusades the knights traveled to the Holy Land with their heavy horses. There they saw Near Eastern warriors mounted on smaller, lighter Arabians and Barbs that were not only fast but agile. After the battles, the Crusaders took many of the light horses home with them to England and France.

When the age of armored knights ended, the Great Horse went to work. The charger that the knights had ridden became the ancestor of the Clydesdale, Percheron, Belgian, Suffolk, and Shire—today's beautiful, strong draft, or work, horses.

THE RETURN
OF THE HORSE

Do you know how horses came back to North America? Christopher Columbus, on his second voyage in 1493, brought them on his ships. The explorers needed pack animals to carry men and supplies. Most horses in America today are descendants of those who came with Columbus, or with the Spaniards in the following years.

In our own West, American Indians hunted buffalo on horseback to provide food for their families. With horses, however, they invaded other tribes' hunting grounds and raided their herds. This led to many tribal wars. The Indians also used horses to push back the settlers from the east.

But settlers kept coming west and building permanent homes. As they did so, they depended on horses more and more. Horses turned forests into farms. They worked in the mines, and hauled the wagons, stagecoaches, and buggies so people could travel from one place to another. They sped through rough mountain passes and across rivers, carrying pouches of mail.

Soon horses were a part of life and everyone had them. Children grew up with horses. The wealthier a family was, the more horses it had. Not too long ago a horse pulling a milk or ice wagon was a familiar sight, and the clanging of a bell meant that a team of puffing horses was speeding down the street hauling a bright red fire engine. You'd see horses and blacksmiths' shops in every town just as you see cars and gas stations today.

WILD HORSES

The only true wild horses are descendants of the animals that early humans couldn't tame. There aren't many alive today. A small, wooly, wild horse lives on the Mongolian plains. It is called Prezwalski's horse, named for a Russian explorer.

Other wild members of the genus *Equus* are the onager of Asia, the wild ass of Africa, who is the ancestor of the donkey, and the wild zebra, also found in Africa.

3

Facts about Horses and Foals

Horses learn by repetition, not by reason. Reward them when they do something right; punish them when they're wrong. Compared with a pig or an elephant, the horse doesn't measure up in brain power. But it can be resourceful at getting into trouble, like opening doors and reaching into the feed bin.

A horse has certain instincts that we don't understand. It can find its way home at night on an unfamiliar trail, and its "sixth sense" for avoiding a cliff or rickety bridge in the dark is well known. So the horse is a very special creature, but not the most intelligent of animals.

Horses do not have a good memory of normal experiences. Training must be repeated over and over until the horse understands what's asked of it. But horses have excellent memories of bad experiences, like bogies on the trail, accidents in the horse trailer, and scary machines.

Horses, like people, have different personalities. There are animals that are spirited and high-strung, geared for action. Others are easygoing and noncompetitive.

The horse may seem cowardly because it runs from danger. But running is an inherited instinct.

THE HORSE'S BODY

A large horse may weigh over 2,000 pounds (908 kg). A small pony can weigh as little as 300 pounds (136 kg). Height is measured in units called *hands.* Many years ago when people wanted to measure a horse's height, they used their hand as a unit of measure. A hand is 4 inches (10 cm). Horses are measured from the ground to the highest point of the *withers*—the top of the horse's shoulders. If a horse measures 62 inches (157 cm), we say it is 15.2 hands high.

The horse's body is covered with a coat of hair. In winter the hair is thick and shaggy. In summer it is smooth. The hair sheds every year.

A big head and a long neck help the horse keep its balance when in motion. It moves its head up and down as it walks and canters, just as we swing our arms when we walk or run. Because the horse's eyes are on the sides of its head, it can see forward, on both sides, and even a little way in back. When a horse canters down a trail, it can see a deer in the field on the left and a robin flying off to the right at the same time. The horse can see better in the dark than we can. It has a sharp sense of hearing and an even sharper sense of smell.

Want to know what a horse is sensing? Watch its ears wiggle. When something up ahead attracts its attention, the horse will point its ears forward. If it detects a voice or movement from be-hind, it will point its ears toward the back. If a horse is annoyed or angry, its ears will flatten back tightly against its neck.

Horses have sharp front teeth that are used for biting grass or other food. The back teeth are for chewing. There is an empty space between these two kinds of teeth. When the horse wears a bridle, the bit fits into this space.

You can tell how old a horse is by looking at the angle of its teeth. A young horse's teeth are straight up and down, and an older horse's teeth point forward.

Horses often snort when they are ridden because they blow air through an empty air pocket inside their noses. The pocket warms the cold air they breathe and makes the snorting sound.

To get rid of pesty flies and mosquitoes, horses shake their heads and manes. The tail is a good swatter, too, when it's swished around. Horses also wriggle their skin to shake off bugs.

Have you ever noticed that horses have stiff whiskers? They act as feelers. About 2 inches (5 cm) long, the whiskers help horses feel the ground when they are grazing, or tell them when they've come to the bottom of their feedbox.

Horses use their soft noses and upper lips to sort through the grass and keep stones or twigs out of their mouths. They pick up grain with their lips, too.

Long legs enable horses to run fast. Most of the horse's weight is carried by its front legs. A horse often sleeps standing up. There is a strong muscle in its neck that supports its head. The horse's leg joints lock to keep its legs from buckling while it sleeps.

Horses grow and mature until they are five years old. Today, many horses live to be twenty. With good care, some hardy animals keep working until well into their thirties.

HORSES' GAITS

The natural *gaits*, or way of going, of a horse are the walk, trot, and canter, or gallop. Each gait has leg and feet movements that follow a pattern. Although these gaits are natural, the horse must learn to perform them in a smooth, rhythmic way.

The slowest gait is the *walk*. The feet are raised one after the other, and are put down in the order in which they were lifted.

The *trot* is bouncy and faster than the walk. When a horse trots, the front and hind legs of opposite sides come to the ground together. This gait makes the horse bend its legs more. But the horse's head remains steady.

Some horses pace instead of trot. When pacing, the front and hind legs on the same side of the body move together. Pacing horses usually are a little faster than trotters in a race.

The slow gallop, or *canter*, is a smooth, rhythmic riding gait. When a horse gallops, one of the forefeet strikes the ground first, then the opposite hind leg strikes the ground, then the other foreleg and hind leg strike the ground together. The horse is either on the right or left lead. For example, if the horse's right legs strike the ground farther forward, it's on the right lead. Around a turn, the horse should lead with its inside legs.

Some horses are trained in gaits other than natural ones. The slow gait is a high-stepping gait done slowly. In the *rack*, a fast, flashy four-beat gait, all four of the horse's feet hit the ground separately. The running walk, sometimes called the Plantation or Tennessee walk, is a comfortable gait somewhere between a walk and a rack. The horse covers a lot of ground quickly and nods its head in time with its hoofbeats.

COLOR IN HORSES

Heredity plays a big part in the color of a horse. If you breed a bay stallion to a bay mare, their offspring will be a bay. A *bay* can vary from reddish brown to dark brown, but the bay always has black *points* (mane, tail, and legs). Reddish-brown horses with black points are called "blood bays."

A gray has a mixture of white and black hair. Grays usually

are born dark and get lighter as they grow older. To be considered a gray, a horse must have at least one gray parent.

There aren't many true white horses. A true white horse is born white. Although an older gray may seem to be a white, it really isn't because it has dark pigment in its skin.

A brown horse may look black but it is not. It has tan or brown hairs on its muzzle and flanks, while all the hairs on a black horse are black.

Dun horses may vary from dark gray to golden. The mane and tail can be almost any color. It may even be a mixture of colors. Sometimes these horses have a back stripe, zebra stripes on their legs, and a little striping over the withers.

Buckskin is a variation of dun, but a buckskin horse has a black mane, tail, and legs, and usually has a back stripe.

A *paint* or *pinto* has white or colored spots or irregular markings on its coat.

A *palomino* is golden or light brown, with a white or cream mane and tail.

Chestnuts can vary from a dark liver color to a pale yellow, with hues of reddish gold. Sorrel is a shade of chestnut. A chestnut's mane and tail can be light or dark, but it is never black. Many times the mane and tail are the exact color of its body.

ABOUT FOALS

A male or female baby horse is called a *foal*. Foals drink their mother's milk. At about six months of age they are separated from their mothers by their owners so they can no longer nurse. We then say they are *weaned*. From the time they are weaned to about age four a male is called a *colt* and a female a *filly*.

Horsepeople consider January 1 to be every horse's birthday. So the first day of the new year, all colts and fillies born the previous year become *yearlings*. When they reach the age of four, colts are called *stallions* and fillies are called *mares*. *Geldings* are males who have been neutered by surgery. Their testes have been removed and the animal can no longer be used for breeding. Geldings usually make better mounts than stallions as they generally are quieter and more dependable.

A FOAL IS BORN

A stallion is the *sire* or father of a foal, and the mare is the *dam*, or mother. When a mare is in foal, for about 330 days—eleven months—the baby horse grows in a sac inside her belly.

Just before the birth, the mare is restless. She may pace the stall, stamp her feet, or begin to sweat. It's time for the foal to be born, so the mother-to-be finds a quiet place and lies down. The foal has been lying on its back inside the sac. Now it turns onto its stomach with its head facing the rear of its mother. The sac with the foal will be pushed down a narrow channel inside the mother by contractions of her abdomen. As the sac comes out it tears and fluid is released.

Slowly the foal's forefeet emerge, with its nose tucked between its legs. Soon the shoulders appear, and then the foal slips right out. This movement rips open the thin sac. But the foal can't separate from its mother yet. They are attached to each other by a birth cord called the umbilical cord. When the foal was inside its mother it was fed through this cord. It will be torn later.

The foal, with some help from the veterinarian, wriggles out of the sac. It's a healthy colt (male). Although it only took about fifteen minutes for his birth, the little foal is tired. He was comfortable inside his mother. Now he is wet and cold.

After he starts breathing, the foal is placed near the mare's head. Mother meets son. She will take care of her little colt just

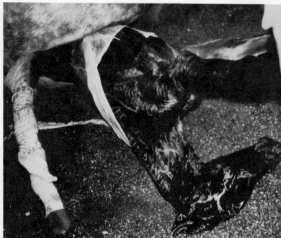

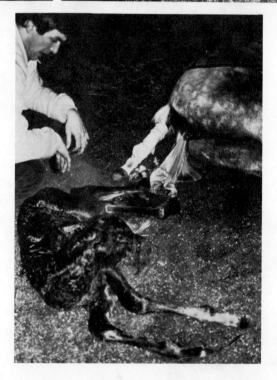

Top left: *as the newborn colt emerges, the fluid-filled sac which contained him within his mother's body is torn.* Top right: *the colt's forefeet emerge first and then his head.* Right: *fully emerged, the colt is still attached to his mother by the umbilical cord.*

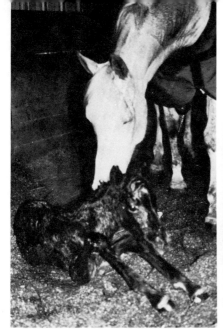

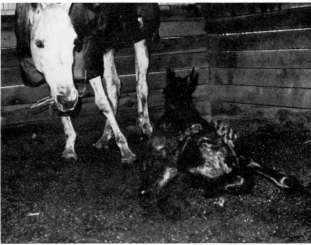

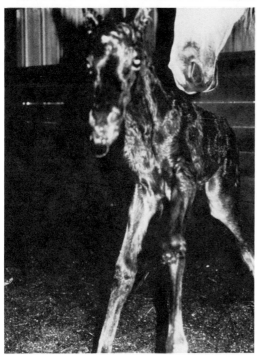

Top left: *the movement of the mare as she licks the colt dry serves to break the umbilical cord and the colt is free.* Top right: *only minutes old, the colt tries to stand but sinks back to the ground.* Left: *on the next try, still a bit wobbly, he makes it.*

as a human mother takes care of her baby. The first thing the mare does is to lick him dry, and her movement usually tears the umbilical cord. Then she cleans his nose so he can breathe better. If people are around, they'll help the mare by rubbing the foal dry with soft towels.

The little colt tries to stand, but he's too weak. He sinks back to the ground. After resting awhile, he raises his head and looks around for his mother. When he smells her, he feels safe.

About half an hour later, the newborn foal tries to stand again. He's stronger now, and although his long legs are still wobbly, it looks as if he'll make it this time.

Look, he did it! He's standing! Although his legs are unsteady, he is actually walking. It takes a human baby about a year to walk alone, but a foal can walk on the day it is born.

When the newborn foal is hungry, he'll suck the milk from his mother's udder. After two or three weeks he may start nibbling grass, but he will still drink his mother's milk. As the new little foal runs at his mother's side, she will feed and protect him and teach him how to get along. In about six months, he'll be weaned and able to feed himself. He'll grow bigger, stronger, and more independent every day until he becomes a handsome stallion.

4

Some Popular Horse Breeds

Do you know why there are so many breeds? It's because we found that some horses were good at doing one thing and some another. There was no one *breed* that could meet all of our needs. The big, powerful horses that came from Europe were calm and even-tempered. They were good at pulling wagons and doing heavy work. The smaller, faster horses, bred mostly in the countries of Asia, were best for riding and racing.

People began to mix these two strains and produce horses for their own special needs. This was the start of what we call "selective breeding." These mixtures produced many different breeds, such as big Clydesdales for heavy work; light, fast horses like Thoroughbreds to run races; and small horses like ponies for children to ride.

Each horse breed has an organization that lists the members and makes the rules for that breed. A horse must be listed with its breed association to be an official member.

The words *purebred* and *Thoroughbred* are often confused. A purebred horse is one that is bred only within one breed. Thoroughbred is the name of a breed of race horses.

A *crossbred* has two parents of different breeds. A *halfbred* has one purebred parent. All purebreds can be *registered*, but there are special rules for registering crossbreds and halfbreds within each breed.

To register a horse, the owner lists it with the headquarters of that particular breed and receives a certificate of registration. The horse's *pedigree* is on the certificate. It gives the names of the sire, dam, and ancestors of the horse, the date of birth, color, and markings. If the owner doesn't know the animal's breeding, then it can't be registered.

THE ARABIAN

The oldest breed of purebred horse, the *Arabian*, originated over two thousand years ago in the deserts of the Middle East. Small and light of build, Arabians measure between 14.1 and 15.1 hands. They may not be big, but these horses are strong and tough from having lived for centuries under difficult conditions. Arabians can carry as much weight as a larger horse.

For hundreds of years, when breeders wanted to improve their horses' *bloodlines*, they bred their animals to Arabians. There is Arabian blood in almost all *light horse* breeds.

Arabians are famous for their *dished faces*, which are slightly curved inward just below the eyes. They have small ears, large jawbones, and delicate muzzles. Because of their slender muscles they can run long distances without getting hot or tired.

Arabians are the oldest breed of purebred horses. They are known for their endurance and longevity as well as their beauty.

The most common Arabian colors are bay and gray. A pure-bred Arabian is never a buckskin, palomino, or pinto. You'll find these colors, though, in part-Arabian horses.

Long ago, nomad desert tribes led hard, wandering lives. Their horses had to be strong, eat very little, and be able to survive in desert heat. During their frequent wars, a well-trained horse could save the life of a Bedouin tribesman, so he treated his horse like a family member. The Arabian war mare often lived in the tent with her owner.

Arabians learn quickly. With patience Arabians can be trained for almost any purpose. They make excellent saddle horses under English or Western *tack*. They are exquisite in the show-ring, are nearly unbeatable on long endurance and competitive trail rides, are used for racing, and for *cutting cattle*. Arabians are also good jumpers. In parade dress with neck and tail arched, nostrils flaring, the Arabian is a beautiful sight.

Some people think Arabians are hard to control. Not true. A well-trained Arabian is as easy to control as any other horse. Arabians live long and often work and breed into their twenties.

PART-ARABIANS

If Arabians are crossbred with other breeds of horses their offspring are called part-Arabian, even if the foal has 75 percent Arabian blood or more. When these horses are registered with the International Arabian Horse Association they are called Half-Arabians. Part-Arabians are often bred in different colors and reach larger sizes than purebreds.

THE BARB

The *Barb* originated in North Africa, in a section that was called the Barbary Coast. It resembles the Arabian in size and build, but it is sturdier and coarser, and its tail is low-set. Unlike the Arabian's dished face, the Barb has a rounded "Roman nose." Barbs are tough and surefooted. Crossbreeding of Arabians and Barbs has produced many excellent horses.

THE MUSTANG

The spirited horses Columbus and the Spanish explorers brought to America had a mixture of Arabian and Barb blood. They were chosen to come to the New World because of their stamina for traveling long, hard distances. Among them were the jennets, splendid light horses. The offspring of many of the Spanish horses were captured by Indians during raids on settlers.

The Spanish horses were the ancestors of the Indians' horses called cayuses. Products of chance breeding, these horses of the western plains were mostly small and scraggly. Yet they were good workers. Spanish cowboys called the cayuses *mestenos*, meaning "wild," or "strayed." American cowboys changed it to *mustangs*.

Our famous western wild mustangs are the descendants of these once-tamed mustangs. They were either abandoned by their owners or they jumped a fence and ran away. The mustangs aren't wild in the sense that other horses whose ancestors were never tamed are, but we still call them wild mustangs.

The mustangs multiplied fast, and by the end of the 1700s they roamed the entire West and as far north as Canada. American Indians, or cowboys who wanted horses to ride, often caught and broke wild mustangs. Those that were caught and tamed became the workhorses of the American West.

Mustangs still run wild today. Some farmers and ranchers have complained because their grazing land is overrun by these horses. They consider mustangs to be worthless because they don't work, they provide no meat, and they can't be ridden. Yet other people think of the wild mustangs as symbols of freedom and independence.

So the government has made laws to protect them. When the herds must be thinned or moved, the horses are rounded up and given to people who volunteer to provide them with good homes. This Adopt-A-Horse Program is run by the United States Department of the Interior's Bureau of Land Management.

THE THOROUGHBRED

Almost three hundred years ago, the Thoroughbred was developed in England. Three *foundation sires*—the Byerley Turk, the Goldolphin Arabian, and the Darley Arabian—were mated with English mares to produce this breed.

Since 1775, when Americans found that in a one-mile (1.6-km) race Thoroughbreds could run twice as fast as most other horses, they imported stock from England and bred their own racing champions.

Thoroughbreds are larger and taller than Arabians and have straight, rather than dished, profiles. The average Thoroughbred is over 16 hands high. People say that this breed gets its speed and stamina from its Arabian ancestors. It takes a well-trained jockey to handle a nervous, competitive Thoroughbred.

Thoroughbreds that aren't fast enough to race are often retrained as show jumpers, dressage horses, steeplechase horses, or three-day-event horses. Others are used in polo matches.

Like the Arabian, the Thoroughbred has been used all over the world to improve horse breeds. Secretariat is an example of a famous racing Thoroughbred. He is a triple crown winner. That's what a horse is called that has won the Kentucky Derby, The Preakness, and the Belmont Stakes—three important races—in one year. No horse could match Secretariat's speed on the race track. Although his racing days are over, the big, beautiful, chestnut stallion lives in Kentucky and is used for breeding. Because racing is a popular sport in America, many owners hope to breed a colt with the grace, speed, and spirit of this superhorse.

The best-known races in America are for two- and three-year-olds, so Thoroughbreds begin training early. A Thoroughbred may have a rider on its back when it's just over a year old.

THE MORGAN

The *Morgan* is one of America's most famous horse breeds. There are different versions of the story of how this breed originated. The most popular is that during the American Revolution a stallion named True Briton was stolen from an English colonel who had come to America to fight the colonists. This horse is credited with being the foundation sire of the breed.

Some time in the late 1700s, Justin Morgan, a poor singing master, walked from his home in Randolph, Vermont to West Springfield, Massachusetts, to collect money owed him by a farmer. The man paid off his debt by giving Morgan two colts. One was big and beautiful, the other a small, scrawny animal sired by the English horse, True Briton.

Morgan sold the large colt, but nobody would buy the little dark bay with the black mane and tail. To earn money, Morgan rented the scrawny colt to farmers and loggers. The little colt earned his feed pulling tree stumps, dragging logs, and helping with plowing. He was a hard worker and never seemed to tire. Morgan entered his horse in several races and pulling contests. He won every time! Morgan's extraordinary horse could outrun and outpull any horse in Vermont, even those twice his size.

The young colt grew to be a small, heavily muscled stallion with a deep and short-backed body, short legs, powerful shoulders, and a full neck. Besides being strong, he had great spirit and smooth gaits. It was hard to believe that after working all day, the little horse still had the energy to win races at night. People called him by his owner's name, "Justin Morgan." His offspring became known as Morgans. The best characteristics of the sire were passed from one generation to another.

Today, there are thousands of registered Morgans. Modern Morgans are more delicate than Justin Morgan because of having Arabian and Thoroughbred blood. Morgans can show, race, jump, or handle stock. They are shown in harness, and used for general work and pleasure riding.

THE AMERICAN
SADDLE HORSE

The American Saddlebred Horse was developed by crossing Arabians, Thoroughbreds, Morgans, and Naragansett Pacers. The result was a tall (15 to 16 hands), graceful horse with a well-shaped head, beautiful long neck, large eyes set wide apart, slim legs, a thick flowing mane and tail, and delicate pointed ears.

Saddlebreds are usually bred as bays, grays, or sorrels with flaxen or dark tails, or as blue-blacks. Besides the natural gaits of walk, trot, and canter, they are often trained to do the slow gait and the rack, making them *five-gaited* horses. No other breed equals the ability of the Saddle Horse to do the flashy rack.

Americans had produced Saddlebred Horses since colonial times, but the breed gained most of its fame during the Civil War (1861–65). Because Saddlebreds were spirited and intelligent and had speed and good balance for quick maneuvers, they were chosen as mounts by famous generals of both the North and the South.

A young American Saddlebred Horse.
Saddlebreds are spirited and fast.

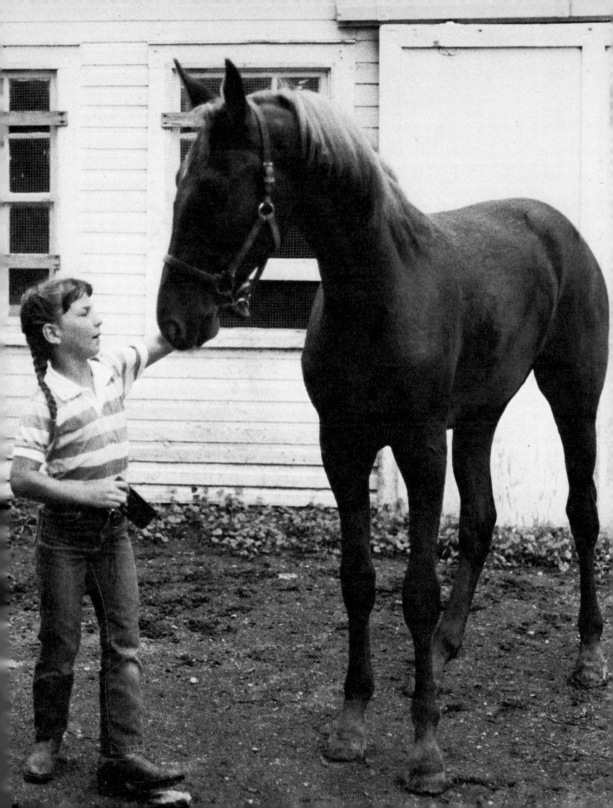

General Grant rode his Saddle Horse, Cincinnati, into battle. General Lee had Traveller; General Sherman's Saddle Horse was Lexington; and General Stonewall Jackson's mount was Little Sorrel. Besides serving as war horses, Saddle Horses worked on farms, raced, and were ridden by farmers and plantation owners.

In 1891, several Saddle Horse breeders formed an organization to encourage better breeding practices. They also established the first horse registry in the United States. This group later became the American Saddle Horse Breeders Association.

For years Saddlebreds were raised and trained mostly for show competition. Many were developed into show-ring champions. That's why the American Saddle Horse is often called "the peacock of the show-ring."

THE STANDARDBRED

In colonial times, people wanted fast-stepping horses to pull their carriages and buggies. So they developed the *Standardbred.* An outstanding English stallion named Messenger was the foundation sire of this breed. He was bred to Norfolk Trotters, mares that could do a fast trot or pace while pulling a rig. They foaled the first American Standardbreds, known as the best trotters in the world.

Often compared to Thoroughbreds, Standardbreds are similiar in color to the racing horse, with an additional dun color. Standardbreds have calmer dispositions, though, and they are smaller, with heavier bodies and shorter legs. When a Standardbred trots, its hind feet reach much farther forward than those of other breeds.

Today, Standardbreds are mainly used in harness racing, where they pull light carts called sulkies. They run two types of races, one at a trot, the other at a pace. In both gaits, for a tiny split second, all four of the horse's feet are off the ground at the same time.

THE TENNESSEE
WALKING HORSE

Nearly two hundred years ago, the Walking Horse was developed in the Tennessee area for plantation owners who wanted a special type of horse to ride while overseeing their land. They needed a mount that could go 40 or 50 miles (64 or 80 km) a day and still give them a fast, comfortable ride.

Four great breeds were blended to start this new horse family: Thoroughbred, Saddlebred, Standardbred, and Morgan. To form a registry, a stallion named Black Allan was selected as foundation sire.

For gentle manners and good disposition the Walking Horse has no equal. It has three natural gaits, but is best known for its comfortable running walk that covers a lot of ground quickly. In the fast, smooth, running walk, the horse moves gracefully, lifting its front feet high and reaching its hind feet several inches in front of where the front feet were set down. The greater the overstride, the faster and smoother the action.

For many years, the Walker was bred and trained mostly for show competition. But today more and more people are enjoying the Tennessee Walker as a pleasure horse. Thoroughbreds run a fast race and their work is over for the day. A Walking Horse can do the running walk for many hours and travel at 6 to 8 miles (10–13 km) an hour. Its relaxing "rocking chair" canter and calm disposition make it a good mount for children as well as for the elderly.

THE AMERICAN
QUARTER HORSE

The American Quarter Horse is a well-known breed that started as a quarter-mile racer in colonial days and developed into a horse

The American Quarter Horse is a short-legged running
horse capable of great speed over short distances.

used for many purposes. Its heavily muscled, powerful hindquarters show where its speed and strength are concentrated.

A typical horse of this breed is medium-sized (14.3 to 15.1 hands) and of stocky build. It has large eyes, alert ears, a short back, deep chest, short neck, and fairly short legs. It runs the range of colors but there are no spotted coats.

The American Quarter Horse was produced long before the Revolutionary War—even before the Thoroughbred was developed in America. Settlers bred their heavy English horses to descendants of the Spanish horses. The result was a strong, short-legged running horse capable of great speed over short distances. These horses were used to round up wild cattle, but wealthy plantation owners also raced them on the main streets of the towns, which were about a quarter of a mile (.4-km) long.

The racehorses were called Quarter Milers or American Quarter Running Horses. Later they became known as *Quarter Horses*. For a long time they were the only racehorses in America.

Then, around 1752, Janus, a Thoroughbred stallion, was brought to the colonies. He had speed and power and sired many offspring. When races were held between Thoroughbreds and Quarter Horses, Quarter Horses won the short races, but Thoroughbreds always won the longer runs.

Eventually racing people lost interest in the short races. The Quarter Horse's useful days were not over, though. It was taken out west to work for the cowboys.

Cowboys liked the Quarter Horse. They said it had "cow sense," an instinct for cutting a calf out of a herd or catching a runaway. The tough Quarter Horse could run over rugged terrain, push through tangled underbrush, swim rivers, and brace itself against a heavy, wild steer at the end of a rope. It was just the kind of horse that was needed on the western frontier.

Modern cowboys like the Quarter Horse, too. It is still the best short-distance runner and a good worker around a western corral. The Quarter Horse makes a fine pleasure horse, too, and is ridden in show competitions and rodeos. This breed is often a favorite of polo players because it is surefooted and can make quick stops and starts, and fast, tight turns. There are more Quarter Horses registered as purebreds than any other breed—more than two million.

5

Draft Horses, Color Breeds, and Others

Just as the mustangs and Quarter Horses were the workhorses of the American West, *draft horses* were the workhorses in the East. These horses, each weighing more than 2,000 pounds (908 kg), pulled plows, dragged logs, and hauled wagonloads on farms.

Yet draft horses weren't always workhorses. They once were the majestic mounts of medieval knights. The big, strong charger wore 200 pounds (91 kg) of armor, as did the knight, and it carried him into battle besides.

There are at least thirty breeds of draft horses. We will discuss six of the most popular breeds: Belgian, Percheron, Clydesdale, Shire, Suffolk Punch, and American Cream.

The Belgian, an old breed, is said to be the strongest of the drafters. It is big and rugged, but has a calm disposition. This handsome horse is usually a chestnut with a flaxen mane and tail and light-colored *stockings*. Because of its short legs, however, it doesn't have high action or an airy way of going. It is slow-moving and built for big tasks. If there is a wagon stuck in the mud, and a tractor can't pull it out, a Belgian will dig in its toes and do the job.

In the United States, Belgians are raised more for exhibition purposes or to take part in pulling contests than to work on farms or in forests.

The Percheron, another giant of the draft breeds, is a spirited horse that originated in the La Perche district southwest of Paris, France. Because it is the only draft horse with Arabian blood, it has a certain beauty not found in other drafters.

Most Percherons are either black or gray, and lift their feet high when trotting. This flashy-looking horse which once pulled the coaches of European nobles is more likely to be found today performing in the circus, being judged in the show-ring or competing in pulling contests.

Bareback circus riders ride only gray Percherons—called rosinbacks because rosin is rubbed into their backs and loins to keep the riders from slipping. The rosin can't be seen by the audience because it blends right into the horses' gray coats.

Clydesdales look like show horses. They have action and stamina, and are seen in pairs or big hitches on farms all over the world. The fine, silky hair below their knees is called "feathers." Clydesdales move along at a jaunty pace, lifting their sturdy legs high, doing their proud, quick gait known as the "heather step."

This handsome drafter with the powerful shoulders and strong, arched neck is the national horse of Scotland. Its name comes from the River Clyde there. Most Clydesdales are bay, black, or brown, and all or part of the leg below the knee is white.

Americans are familiar with these horses because we've seen the Anheuser-Busch Company's outstanding teams at fairs, shows, parades, and on television.

English Shires and Suffolk Punches are not as popular in the United States as other drafters, yet they are important. The English Shire is the biggest drafter (often more than 17 hands high) but it

Percherons, smallest of the draft breed, were once used to pull the coaches of European nobles. Today they are more likely found performing in the circus or competing in pulling contests.

lacks refinement. It is used as a workhorse in the forests and on farms in the marshlands of England.

The English say that because the Shire has the biggest horseshoe it brings the most luck. You can find the Shire's shoe hanging over many an English barn door.

The Suffolk Punch, claimed to be the oldest of draft breeds, is part of the history of eastern England. Suffolks' coats come in seven different shades of chestnut. A typical Suffolk Punch has a flaxen or cream-colored mane and tail, and it may have a touch of white on its nose or heels. It is not as hairy as other breeds and always looks as if it has just been clipped.

Because this drafter used to have a plumpness that the English call "punched up," it was named the Suffolk Punch. Modern Suffolks still have powerful, muscular bodies, but they've lost the barrel look. When pulling a heavy load, a good team of Suffolks will drop to its knees and tug and drag until the job is done.

The American Cream was developed in central Iowa in the early 1900s. The ideal Cream has pink skin with white markings, amber eyes, and white mane and tail. Recognized as a breed in 1950, this drafter has beauty, a good disposition, style in the show-ring, and is a willing farm worker.

COLOR HORSES

Horses come in many different colors and combinations of colors. In certain breeds, all animals are the same color. For instance, all Suffolk Punches are chestnuts, and Percherons are either gray or black. Most of the time, though, the color of a horse is not a trait of the breed.

People choose horses with colors they like best. Some like white horses or golden palominos. Others may prefer spotted horses or buckskins. When colors are especially popular, owners have formed organizations to register their horses.

Even though they are registered, color breeds are not the same as true breeds. A horse may be a registered palomino but it can also be a Quarter Horse or a mixed breed. Color registries have rules about which breeds can be registered. Some popular American color breeds are the Appaloosa, palomino, pinto, the American White Horse, and buckskin.

The *Appaloosas* have an interesting history. Brought to the New World by Spanish explorers, they were acquired by the Nez Percé peoples of Northwest America in the early 1700s. The Nez Percés bred the best horses—those with speed, stamina, and good spotted coats. Eventually a horse was produced that was fast, tough, and surefooted.

The majority of the Appaloosas in America belonged to the Nez Percés until the end of the Nez Percé War of 1877 when Chief Joseph's band surrendered to government troops. The herd was then sold off and dispersed.

Sixty years later, interest in the breed was rekindled, and a search was mounted for any horse with Appaloosa characteristics for inclusion in the registry.

Appaloosas have a light-and-dark pattern, especially on their faces. Their eyes have a white area, or sclera, around the dark iris, just as we do. Hooves are striped up and down. Most of the time a large front area of the body is one color while the rear part is white with dark, irregular spots. The Appaloosa's mane and tail tend to be rather thinly haired.

You might think the name *Appaloosa* is Indian, but it's French. It comes from the Palouse River area where the Indians raised their spotted horses. French traders and trappers said it was "a Palousey" horse, which soon became Appaloosa.

Appaloosas are said to be "easy keepers." They work on ranches, are shown in competition, ridden in rodeos, and used for pleasure riding. An Appaloosa in a parade is a colorful sight, especially if the rider is dressed as a cowboy or nineteenth-century Indian.

Palominos are a popular color breed. Some palominos are a beautiful golden color, with a white or almost-white mane and tail. Others are almost brown. Since the palomino's characteristics are inherited from its Arabian and Thoroughbred ancestors, there are those that are big and powerful, and those that are small and light. Heavy palominos are used for handling stock. They are shown under Western tack and are ridden in rodeos. Lightweights work on ranches, too, and are shown under English tack and in harness classes. They are also used for jumping and in polo. But lightweight or heavyweight, a palomino makes a handsome parade horse.

Pinto and paint horses have several things in common with palominos. They are classified by color, have Arabian ancestors, vary a lot in size and weight, and were brought to the New World by Spanish explorers. The story goes that Spanish stallions escaped from explorers, mated with native ponies, and produced the pintos and paints of the West. Showy, obedient, easy to handle, good under English or Western tack, they are used as parade mounts and for pleasure riding and handling stock.

The name *pinto* comes from the Spanish word *pintado,* which means "painted," or "mottled." Can you guess why Indians of the West liked pintos or paints? It was because their color patches broke up the horse's outline and it was hard for their enemies to see them.

Today paints and other breed types can be registered with the Pinto Horse Association. Yet the American Paint Association will register only pintos with Quarter Horse or Thoroughbred conformation.

The pinto is believed to be descended from the mating of
Spanish stallions and native ponies of the American West.

The buckskin is one of the original color patterns of primitive horses. The body is a shade of yellow, ranging from pale gold to almost brown. The lower legs, mane, and tail are black or dark brown. To be a registered buckskin, a horse must have these traits. Sometimes a buckskin has a dark stripe down its back and it may have another stripe running across its shoulders from side to side. The black on its legs breaks up into stripes near the knees.

The American White Horse, formerly called the American Albino, was always considered to be special. Long ago, people worshipped the regal white horse, and it was a favorite of kings and queens. To be registered in the American White Horse Association, a horse must be born white, with white hair, pink skin, and blue, brown, or hazel eyes. Because the White Horse looks well in costume and can be trained to perform, many have been chosen to work in circuses.

THE PASO FINO

The Paso Fino is a beautiful, smooth-gaited breed. Spirited under saddle, this light horse has been around a long time, but recently it has become more popular.

The horses Columbus brought to the New World were a mixture of Barb, Andalusian, and Spanish jennet blood. They were selectively bred to other Spanish horses brought to the Americas later on. The Paso Fino is the result of the blending of these breeds.

You can find Paso Finos in every color, with or without white markings. Not big (13 to 15.2 hands), this horse often doesn't grow to its full size until its fifth year. Its head and ears are short, and ears generally curve inward at the tip. The eyes are widely spaced and large.

All Paso Finos are born with a natural, four-beat lateral (side) gait. It is performed at three speeds. Paso Finos can also walk as other horses do, and many can perform a collected canter and a relaxed lope as well.

The Paso Fino was first used in war, then in exloring and developing the New World. Today, its beauty and unique style not only makes it a winner in the show-ring, it's a comfortable mount on long trail rides, and it performs well in the rodeo or when working with cattle.

THE MINIATURE HORSE

Although Miniature Horses are small (no larger than 8.2 hands), they are not considered ponies. Some Miniatures are built like stocky draft horses, others have the fine bones of Thoroughbreds.

Miniatures are the result of selective breeding over the past one hundred years. The first Miniature Horses in the United States were used in the coal mines of Virginia in the late 1880s.

Many United States breeders are raising Miniature Horses. They are popular because they make excellent backyard pets for children. A space as small as 5 sq. ft. (.465 sq m) is adequate for these little horses, but they must be exercised every day.

The average foal attains most of its height when it's one year old, and is a full-grown adult at two. Miniatures live long—thirty-five to forty years. They don't require as much feed as large horses do, and are less expensive to keep. They can be trained to do almost any trick a bigger horse can do. Miniatures are often seen pulling small wagons in parades and at fairs.

THE LIPIZZANER

The *Lipizzaner*, a big, powerful, white horse, is known for its courage and intelligence. As graceful as a ballet dancer, it performs difficult dressage routines to classical music.

This old, pure breed originated in Imperial Austria in the late sixteenth century. Emperor Maximilian II imported Arabian stallions and bred them to Spanish mares. Their offspring became the white Lipizzaners, named for the town of Lipizza where they were foaled. Only stallions were trained at the Spanish Riding School on the palace grounds in Vienna. Even today, mares live with their foals, but are not ridden.

Foals are born a dark brown color; they become gray at four; and between seven and ten years of age, they turn pure white.

Colts receive no training until the age of four. Then they are sent to school to learn manners, rhythm, and acrobatics. The training goes slowly for the next two or three years, and the colt is carefully watched at every stage to evaluate his progress. Many are weeded out.

The strongest, most intelligent stallions are taught to perform the difficult *dressage* movements. Horse and rider must know all the signals (called aids) and perform as if they are one.

The stallion is taught many movements, each with another degree of difficulty, requiring more concentration from the trainer and more strength and balance from the horse.

Only horses with thick, powerful legs are chosen to learn the leaping steps called "airs." Some Lipizzaner schooling ends here, but there are still the ultimate movements, the courbette and the capriole, for the most outstanding stallions.

During World War II (1939–45) war threatened the Spanish Riding School. But General George Patton of the U.S. Army or-

Lipizzaners are known for their grace and intelligence. The best are taught to perform complicated classical movements known as dressage.

dered a special mission to keep the Soviets from capturing the horses, and furnished a convoy of armored tanks to bring back the mares and foals the Nazis had hidden in Czechoslovakia. When General Patton was killed, General Mark Clark ordered the stallions to be brought to a town in the American zone of Austria where the Spanish Riding School could continue its work.

In 1950 Americans saw the famous Lipizzaners when they performed in New York. Eight years later, Tempel Smith imported twenty Viennese Lipizzans to his farm in Wadsworth, Illinois, and founded what is now the largest herd of Lipizzaners in the world. After Smith's death, a center was established for these horses to give public performances. A staff of national experts in fields such as classical music, staging, and choreography put together a lively production. The Spanish Riding School in Vienna, and Tempel Farms in Wadsworth, Illinois, are the only two schools in the world that teach purebred Lipizzaners the ancient art of classical dressage.

TRAKEHNER

Polish horses are gaining popularity in the United States. Long ago, at Trakehnen, a stud farm in Poland (later part of East Prussia and now in East Germany), a bloodline was started by breeding heavy war horses to hardy native stock.

When Poland was partitioned in 1772, all important breeding centers in East Prussia came under the control of Germany. Near the end of World War II, when the Soviet Army advanced toward the area, the Germans fled, taking with them about a thousand of the best of Poland's oldest, most-prized horse breed, the Trakehner.

Today, the Trakehner is being claimed by both countries. According to a 1732 law of Trakehnen, only horses bred and foaled there can be called Trakehners. Yet experts say that all Trakehners' bloodlines can be traced to the original stud farm.

Because of new interest in these expensive animals in the United States, Poles and Germans and others are still debating which country is breeding the true Trakehner. Despite the debate, the export of Trakehners from both countries continues.

Many farms in the United States now specialize in breeding the powerful Trakehner. This horse, with the blood of cavalry chargers, graceful Polish horses, Thoroughbreds, and Arabians, is used here in show competitions and for hunting and jumping.

6

Ponies

Ponies are not young horses. A *pony* is actually a smaller grown-up member of the horse family and it, too, is a descendant of Eohippus, the Dawn Horse. Any adult horse, other than Miniatures, not more than 14.2 hands at the withers is called a pony. Ponies are not all just small horses, some are members of specific breeds.

Ponies have small, wide, strong bodies, short legs, and muscular necks. Many have beautiful, thick manes and tails. They developed in cold parts of the world, either in the mountains or on northern islands where there wasn't much grazing land. Because of the cold and the scarcity of food, these animals never grew to be the size of horses living in milder climates. Yet ponies are survivors and live longer than other horses do. Many live to be forty years old.

If you like ponies, joining a Pony Club is one way to meet others who like ponies, too.

There are many breeds of ponies. One of the best known is the Shetland, a native of the Shetland Isles in Great Britain. The Shetland is the smallest breed, so tiny it is measured in inches instead of hands. Looking like a miniature draft horse, the Shetland has a stocky, barrel-shaped body, heavy neck, thick forelock and mane, and shaggy winter coat.

This little horse worked for the islanders, hauling peat for fuel and sacks of seaweed to fertilize small farms. It was hard work, but if there was a storm, the farmer would take his pony inside the cottage and keep it warm and dry.

In 1840, when a law was passed outlawing women and children working in the mines, the Shetland replaced them. Ponies hauled coal cars through dark, low-roofed passageways. Some of the pit ponies never came up to breathe fresh air.

When the mines were electrified, there was no longer a need for the pit pony. Early in the 1900s, the islanders sent Shetlands to America to be children's ponies.

North American breeders developed another taller, slimmer Shetland with a prettier head. Although it is still a child's horse, the American Shetland is a high-stepping show pony, often driven in harness. It is considered to be a separate breed from the Shetland Islands Pony.

Another beautiful old breed is the Welsh Pony. With its graceful head, large, dark eyes, delicate muzzle, long mane, and full tail, it looks like a tiny Arabian. There is a legend that Arabian stallions from wrecked ships of the Spanish Armada swam to Wales and mated with native wild ponies to start this breed.

In America today, Welsh Ponies are divided into two groups. Those no taller than 12.2 hands (50 inches [127 cm]) and larger ponies up to 14.2 hands (58 inches [147 cm]). Welsh Ponies are spirited mounts and make good pleasure horses and jumpers for young people. Many children move up to the Welsh Pony when they grow too big for the Shetland. The larger Welshes are strong and fast and can be ridden until riders are about sixteen years of age.

You may have read *Misty of Chincoteague,* Marguerite Henry's famous book. It is a fascinating tale of the wild ponies that live off the coast of northern Virginia on the small island of Assateague. These ponies have inhabited the island for over three hundred years. Nobody really knows how they got there.

Every summer since 1925, there is a special event called Pony Penning Day. Cowboys round up the wild ponies of Assateague and drive them into the sea. The ponies—large, small, solid colored, and pintos—swim across the narrow channel to nearby Chincoteague. To thin out the herd, the youngest animals (because they are trainable) are sold at auction. Overpopulation would cause many of the ponies to starve. After the sale, the mares and stallions are driven back to their home island.

The young person who owns one of these ponies will have a good riding pony after it is tamed and trained.

The Connemara Pony was bred in the hills of western Ireland. We don't know its exact origin, but this pony, the largest of the native breed (13 to 15 hands), had to have strong ancestors that gave it the stamina to survive the frequent Atlantic storms, and help it to stay alive in the rugged Irish countryside.

Connemaras are capable of carrying an adult in the hunting field, and yet they are gentle enough for a young child. They are easy to train in dressage, famous for show jumping, and are an excellent choice for driving events. This versatile animal can pull a buggy or a sleigh, go trail riding, or be a backyard pet.

In 1956, the American Connemara Pony Society was formed. American ponies are bred in a milder climate with better pasture

Top: *according to legend, Welsh Ponies are descendents of Arabian stallions that mated with the native wild ponies of Wales.* Bottom: *the Connemara Pony is famous for show jumping.*

MONROE JUNIOR HIGH SCHOOL LIBRARY
MONROE, MICHIGAN

than the original Irish ponies, but they have retained the sure-footedness and natural jumping ability of their ancestors.

A comparatively new breed, the Pony of the Americas, or POA, is the first Western-style pony bred for children and small adults to ride. This gentle but strong pony, with its spotted coat, looks like an Appaloosa. It has become popular because it is easy to get along with and has a smooth way of going. The breed was produced by mating Appaloosas, Arabians, and Quarter Horses with Shetland or Welsh Ponies. To be a registered POA, a pony must have at least one POA parent and show Appaloosa traits.

Another breed gaining popularity in America is the Norwegian Fjord Pony. You can ride, drive, hunt, and jump a Fjording. Although this breed is relatively new to America, selective breeding began over four thousand years ago in Norway. The Fjordings are good-looking, with broad foreheads, large eyes, and small ears. They are stocky and powerful, with muscular bodies and short, sturdy legs. All Fjordings are dun colored (tan, cream, or golden) with a full dorsal stripe and black down the center of a silver or flaxen tail. Colts will grow to 14.2 hands at four years old. Fillies are somewhat smaller and lighter. The Norweigan Fjord is big and strong enough to pull a plow, drag logs, or be ridden and driven by adults as well as children.

There are many other popular pony breeds, such as the Dartmoor, bred on the moors of southwestern England; the Highland Pony of Scotland, a gentle, sturdy, surefooted jumping pony; the Haflinger, a pretty, hardy, mountain pony used as a workhorse; and the Hackney Pony from England, famous for its high-stepping trot, and in demand as a harness pony.

People choose to own ponies because they are good family horses. They are strong and can do all kinds of work. They eat less, take less space to board than larger horses, and they are gentle, comfortable mounts for children and small adults.

7

Your First Horse

If you are a beginning rider who is thinking about buying a horse, it's a good idea to take horsemanship and riding lessons first. You'll become a better rider and learn about horses. To show that you can accept the responsibility of owning a horse, help pay for your lessons. Save money from your allowance, birthday gifts, and baby-sitting jobs, or get a part-time job after school. Perhaps a nearby stable will let you do chores, answer phones, or run errands in return for lessons.

Talk to experienced horse owners and ask their advice. Owning a horse is a long-term commitment in time, energy, and money. You must really love horses and riding. Yet ownership can bring you a great deal of pleasure if you have an idea beforehand of how much it will cost. Don't let your fun be spoiled by unexpected expenses after you've taken the big step. The purchase price of the horse is just the beginning. Housing, feeding, shoeing, veterinarian bills, and the tack and tools you must buy add up to a lot more.

Costs will vary according to where you live. Before you go horse shopping, visit several nearby stables and inquire about their facilities, care, and monthly board charge. They are listed in the classified section of your phone book. If you're going to stable at home, check with a feed store as to how much your feed bill might be every month.

Find out what the local farrier (blacksmith) charges. You'll need a visit every six or eight weeks to keep your horses's hooves in shape and to reset or replace worn shoes.

Add in the cost of a veterinarian at least twice a year for worming, innoculations, and floating (filing) your horse's teeth. Check a saddle shop for prices of equipment. You'll need the following: a saddle and bridle, halter and lead rope, a horse sheet or blanket, grooming tools, and first aid supplies. Don't forget your riding clothes and lessons. Add up the costs. Then check with your parents about the financial end of buying a horse.

If you are going ahead with the project, it's a good idea to have an experienced horseperson go with you to examine the prospects for soundness. Don't be in a hurry to buy. There are plenty of horses for sale. Shop around, see what's available in your area, and compare prices.

WHICH HORSE
SHOULD YOU CHOOSE?

Not just any old nag. The right horse for you depends on your age, build, riding experience, and dependability. Before you make a choice, ask yourself what your horse will be used for.

If you are buying a horse for pleasure riding along a forest trail, in a city park, or across farmland, it should be gentle, sound, dependable, and have smooth gaits. Think about a pony, or a *grade horse,* one of mixed breed with good basic training. Even if you plan to show in pleasure classes a few times a year, you'd be better off with a good trail horse that's fun to ride instead of an expensive, high-strung show horse.

If you are an advanced rider and your main interest is showing in pleasure classes, consider a purebred that's primarily used for that class. Whatever breed you choose, the horse must be sound, responsive, have good conformation, and be schooled for the show-ring. Will you jump your horse? Then look for a long-legged hunter type that knows how to jump and won't stumble and fall. Your best bet is probably a Thoroughbred or Part-Thoroughbred. Are you interested in competitive events such as roping, barrel racing, or games on horseback? You'll probably choose a Quarter Horse. Do you want a horse with stamina for endurance riding? You might pick an Arabian.

It's twice as hard and often frustrating to work with a horse that isn't suited for what you want it to do. There are good horses in every breed and if you take your time, you'll find the right horse for you. Sometimes not having the right horse is worse than not having a horse at all.

HOW MUCH WILL YOUR HORSE COST?

You've done your homework—you know how much you and your parents can afford. Horses can be bought for almost any amount, but, like most things, you get what you pay for. The price of a horse varies according to age, breeding, and schooling. If all things are equal, an *aged* horse usually costs less than a younger one, and a grade horse is less than a purebreed.

Beware of a horse that seems too cheap. There's probably a reason for it. A beautiful palomino gelding was for sale that looked much more expensive than the asking price. A new rider bought him and later found that the horse had several bad habits, including kicking every horse and person around him. The palomino was a bad deal for an inexperienced rider at any price.

Expect to pay from a few hundred dollars to two thousand dollars for a grade horse with basic training, according to where you live. If you want a fine animal for racing, show, or breeding, with good bloodlines and schooling, the price will start around two thousand dollars and go perhaps as high as fifty thousand dollars or more, depending on how much winning you expect to do. Since this is your first horse, you don't have to buy an expensive show animal. You may not win many blue ribbons, but your horse will teach you responsibility, patience, and good sportsmanship. Keep in mind, though, that it costs as much to keep a poor horse as it does to keep Secretariat. A dud usually ends up costing more in vet bills and training and it could even be unsafe to ride. Horses live a long time. You'll get your money's worth the longer you keep the animal.

WHERE CAN YOU BUY A HORSE?

Where you buy a horse depends on where you live. If you live on a farm or in a ranch area, it's easy to find a horse for sale. Tell your friends and neighbors that you are looking for a horse. Horsepeople usually know of horses that are available.

If you live in the city, a nearby riding stable may know of a good horse for you. When you buy from a riding academy sometimes you can rent the horse and try it before you buy. Watch out for the seller that rushes you by saying, "Make up your mind right now. Someone is coming to look at this horse tomorrow."

You might ask other horsepeople to give you the names of dealers and breeding farms where they have had good experiences. Usually a dealer who has been in business for a long time is reliable.

Don't buy at a horse auction unless you are with an experienced person who knows horses and can judge them quickly. Horses at auctions are sold to the highest bidder and the sale goes fast. There is no way of telling if the animal is sound.

Another way to find horses for sale is to check the newspapers. If an advertisement says that the owner is selling the horse because he or she is going away to school, that could be a good deal. But if it says "Horse for an experienced rider," look out! It probably means the horse is hot-tempered and hard to handle.

CONFORMATION AND SOUNDNESS

The horse you choose must have good conformation and be sound. *Conformation* (the way a horse is put together) is important, because it influences the horse's ability to hold up when you work it. A sound horse is a healthy horse without injury or weaknesses that may keep it from performing well or make it go lame. You'll want a well-built, balanced animal with smooth gaits and a pleasing appearance.

A horse is only as good as its feet and legs. If the legs are weak, crooked, or poorly formed, they will probably go bad with use and the horse will be lame and worthless. There is a difference, though, between unsoundness and a blemish. An unsoundness, such as crooked legs, impairs the horse's action and usefulness. A blemish, such as a scar from an injury, isn't pretty, but it doesn't interfere with the horse's action and ability to work without going lame.

Don't buy a horse just because it's a pretty color. We all like a good-looking horse, but you are not entering your mount in a beauty pageant. A sound horse that's just been shipped in from a breeding farm or auction can seem thin and sickly. All it may need is some good food to cover its ribs. Frequent grooming will give any dull-looking horse a glossy coat. Keeping the mane, fetlocks, and whiskers trimmed can make an unkempt horse look loved and well cared for. So look beyond the exterior beauty of a horse.

When judging conformation study the horse while its moving as well as standing still. It should have a good way of going and travel with its legs moving in straight lines. Lameness and other unsoundness often show up more when the horse is moving. Again, an experienced horseperson is helpful here.

IS SCHOOLING
IMPORTANT?

You bet it is! Unless you are an advanced rider and have had experience with many types of mounts, don't buy a *green horse* (one without training) that doesn't know any more than you do. Green horses and green riders are a bad combination. Choose a horse that has had some good general training. When you buy a schooled horse you can concentrate on becoming a better rider, not on training the horse. After you've developed yourself as a rider, you may want the fun of training a colt or filly.

WHAT ABOUT
TEMPERAMENT?

Temperament is another important consideration—yours and the horse's. Some people ride with strong legs and hands. Others ride with a loose rein and a light touch. Which type are you? It's more enjoyable to have a mount that wants to work for you, whose basic nature is compatible with your way of riding.

If you're inexperienced, don't buy a hot, hard-to-manage mount. One new rider chose a beautiful, but nervous, racehorse, thinking that with practice he would be able to control it. The horse bolted every time it heard a loud noise, and the owner became a tense, defensive rider. He spent all his time and energy trying to control his mount. If you buy a horse that is too hard for you to manage, it will take the fun out of riding. You want a playmate and friend, a safe horse to ride. Having a smooth, well-mannered horse says more about your horse I.Q. than just controlling a hot horse.

Mares are gentle but touchy. If you don't want to breed your horse, consider a gelding. Geldings are usually calm and dependable, and make good mounts. A new rider should not buy a stallion. Stallions are too strong and excitable for beginners, and besides, they're forbidden on most forest preserve trails.

WHAT AGE HORSE
IS BEST?

Horses are considered full-grown at about four years old, and are called aged at ten. Your first horse should be between five and thirteen years old; around seven or eight is ideal. Under five, the horse is likely to be green and partially schooled. Don't choose a yearling, or a two-year-old—you'd have to wait too long to ride it, and it would cost just as much to keep as a horse you can ride now. A thirteen-year-old horse has at least five good years of riding left. A horse much older than thirteen might be well trained, but apt to have health problems.

WHAT SIZE HORSE
SHOULD YOU GET?

Horses are trained to respond to the pull of reins and pressure of the rider's legs and heels. If you are small and ride a big horse, you won't be able to signal your mount if your legs stick straight out over the horse's sides. Big horses are also difficult for small people to mount and dismount. On the other hand, don't buy a horse so tiny that you'll outgrow it in no time. It's too expensive to buy a new horse every year.

If you're tall and choose a small horse, your legs may hang down below the horse's belly. You'd have to be a contortionist to signal your horse. A medium-sized horse (from 15 to 16 hands) is best for most new riders.

8

When You've Found the Horse You Want

Try to learn your new horse's past history. Who was the former owner? For how long? Why did he or she sell? Is the horse easy to catch? Does it bridle easily? Will it pick up all four feet for cleaning? Ask your knowledgeable horseperson friend to look at it.

Walk and trot the animal on a lead line. Is it gentle? Is it quiet while being groomed and worked around? Does it have clear, alert, kind eyes? How are the feet and legs? Is the horse breathing normally or taking in great gulps of air?

If you are convinced—and your experienced friend agrees—that it's the horse for you, ride it in the ring and later on the trail. Can you control it? Will it stand still after you stop it? Like people, horses have bad habits. The horse may toss its head, chew the bit, or *shy*. It's better to know how a horse acts before you own it. The good traits must outweigh the bad. Ask a more experienced rider to ride it and give an opinion.

Have the horse examined by a veterinarian other than the seller's. The vet will check the horse's eyes, teeth, heart, breathing, and legs for soundness, with the purpose you want to use it for in mind.

When the veterinarian says the animal is sound and you have agreed on the price, ask the seller to let you try the horse for a week or two before you pay. If the seller won't or can't do it, then ask for a guarantee for a certain length of time, say one month, as to the horse's soundness. Don't buy the horse if the seller won't give you that. When the seller agrees, and you've made a satisfactory arrangement, you can go ahead with an easy mind.

WHERE WILL YOU KEEP YOUR HORSE?

You will need a place for your horse. It doesn't have to be fancy, just clean and dry. You can either board it at a nearby riding stable, house your horse in a neighbor's barn and care for it, or keep it at home.

If you are going to board it at a stable, you should have contacted stables earlier, learned costs and availability, visited several, and chosen one that is reasonably clean, with roomy, well-bedded box stalls. An indoor riding arena is an added plus. Since horses like to run and kick up their heels, there should also be an outdoor *paddock* or *corral.*

Ask yourself these questions: Are the owner and hired help friendly? Friendly people who like horses usually treat them well. Do the other horses look cared for? Is there a competent riding instructor at the stable? Pick the kind of place where your parents won't mind you spending a lot of time.

If you are going to stable the horse at home, you'll need a clean, dry, barn to protect it against extreme cold, wind, and heat. There should be an exercise pen or corral. A pasture for summer grazing is ideal. Stabling at home will give you the opportunity to be with your horse every day. You'll learn to know and trust each other.

Before you bring your horse home, make sure that the stall is safe. Remove all nails and smooth off any sharp corners. It should be roomy (at least 100 square feet [9.3 sq m]), well drained, and clean. Wood shavings or straw makes good bedding. See that you replace it when it's dirty. Horses like to be clean just as we do.

Keep your fences strong and in repair. Your neighbors will not like your horse visiting them uninvited.

Your barn should have a room with a concrete floor for storing feed and bedding. Perhaps you'll get a cat to help keep rodents out. A small tack room is a good idea, too. Close it off so your bridles and saddles and other equipment will stay clean.

When you bring your new horse home, remember that everything is strange to it. Don't ride immediately. Give the animal a few days to get used to you and the new surroundings.

You can have the manure picked up, or tie it up in plastic bags and sell it for fertilizer. But the best idea is a compost heap. Make a layer of several inches of leaves or weeds or any dry material, then a layer of manure. Build it up with several alternating layers, keeping a hollow in the top for rain to collect in. Pack it down and let it decay. You could have a cubic yard (.765 cu m) of rich topsoil in a year.

FEEDING YOUR HORSE

Find out what the previous owner fed your horse and if it has allergies. Put the grain in a feedbox. Usually horses are fed crushed or rolled oats along with hay. Horses like variety in their diet, just as we do, but add to or change your horse's regular diet slowly, to avoid painful and often fatal stomach upset (colic). Crushed or soaked barley, bran, or pellets will be readily consumed, but keep portions small. Pellets are a shaped food that contain hay, grain, minerals, and vitamins. A little corn, especially in winter, is a

warming addition to the regular feed. Horses like treats, too, of carrots, apples, and pears. Don't hand-feed them, though, because the horse may nip your finger or kick if it doesn't get the treat.

How much will you feed your horse? It depends on size, appetite, and the amount of work it does. Experience is your best guide, but consult your veterinarian. Horses are like people—some require more food; some eat too much and get fat. It's no pleasure to ride a fat horse. It tends to be lazy. Yet horses shouldn't be bony, either.

Two regular feedings a day, morning and night, are enough under most circumstances. Most adult horses require 1.5 pounds (680 g) of good quality hay per 100 pounds (45 kg) of body weight; for the average 1,000-pound (454-kg) horse, that is about 15 to 20 pounds (7 to 9 kg) of hay a day. Give your horse more food if it works, less if it doesn't. Horses will eat until they get sick, so keep the oats locked up. Always measure by weight the amount of grain you feed; a coffee can of oats weighs much less than a coffee can of cracked corn. If your horse doesn't want to eat, add molasses or honey to its feed.

Hay helps a horse digest its food—it's the roughage or bulk in the diet. Hay also gives the horse something to do instead of chewing the fence. Good hay should be clean and sweet smelling, never dusty or moldy. The most common kinds of hay are timothy, alfalfa, and clover.

Outdoors, use a hayrack or put the hay in a clean hay box in the corral, not on the ground, as nutritious hay leaves may be tramped into the ground. Inside the stall, place the hay near a hanging water bucket. Horses like to dunk the hay in their buckets.

A hayrack keeps the hay off the ground, helping to preserve its nutritional value.

Hay can catch fire quickly. Put up a No Smoking sign in your barn. Don't allow anyone to use matches in or around the barn, tack, or feed room. Inspect electrical wiring frequently for fraying that causes most barn fires.

You'll need a salt block in the feedbox. A horse will lick as much as an ounce (28 g) of salt per day. Horses drink a lot of water—especially in hot weather. They usually drink after eating, so good clean water should be available at all times. Rubber buckets attached to the stall are safe and lasting, but clean them frequently. Water can be carried, piped, or hosed in, or you can use an automatic watering fountain.

GROOMING
YOUR HORSE

Grooming means combing, brushing, and rubbing your horse. It takes time and energy, but it's necessary to keep your horse in good condition. Grooming is a special time for you to get to know your horse and for the animal to become familiar with your touch.

Groom every day if you can, but always before every ride. Regular brushing and cleaning not only soothes tired muscles, it keeps the horse's oil and sweat glands open and working properly and puts a natural gloss on its coat.

Place your horse in the crossties. These are chains or ropes that hook onto each side of the halter from a wall or post. You'll need this equipment: rub rag, sponge, rubber currycomb, dandy brush, body brush, hoof pick, sweat scraper, and a tail and mane comb. The tools are inexpensive, considering what it costs to keep a horse, so get the best.

Combing the mane

Most horses enjoy being groomed and will stand quietly. Begin by wiping the coat with a towel to remove the top dust. Then, to *curry* your horse, use the currycomb. Start just behind the ears on the side of the neck, and rub in circles everywhere but the horse's legs and head. The currycomb loosens the dirt. Most horses like a brisk rubbing, but if your horse has a tender skin, use gentle motions. Every few seconds tap the currycomb against the heel of your shoe or against the wall to knock off the dirt that has collected.

As soon as you've scrubbed the dirt to the surface, sweep it away with the dandy brush you hold in your other hand. Every few strokes, clean the brush with the currycomb.

Clean and brush the mane and tail with the special comb and the dandy brush. Brush the mane thoroughly. Flip it over and brush the underside, too. Finish brushing on the right side of the neck. Then use the mane comb. If the hair is badly tangled, separate it first with your fingers. Now use the body brush over the entire horse. Brush in the direction that the hair grows. Finish by wiping the horse with a clean cloth. The coat should shine like satin.

Don't forget to wipe your horse's eyes and the area around its tail with damp cotton or a clean damp sponge.

Pick the feet with a hoof pick. It's a safe tool and does a good job. Start with the near forefoot. Facing the horse's tail, put your left shoulder against the animal's left shoulder. Now slide your hand down the tendons behind the cannon bone, and at the same time lean against the horse's shoulder to throw its weight onto its opposite front foot. Tell the horse, "Lift your foot." As soon as the horse does so, continue sliding your left hand down until the hoof

*Use a hoof pick to clean out
small stones and dirt that collect
in crevices of the horse's feet.*

is cradled in your hand. Bend the fetlock joint as much as you can to turn the bottom of the foot upward, in a flat position.

Your horse should get used to having its feet picked up. If you don't know how to do it, ask someone who is experienced to show you.

To pick the feet, start at the heel and work toward the toe. Clean out small stones, dirt, and manure that collect in the crevices, and about the *frog,* the pad in the middle of the sole of the foot. When you're finished, put the foot down gently. Clean your horse's feet every day and before and after riding.

After you work your horse, cool it off and groom it again. The second grooming is relaxing. The horse's sweat brings the dirt to the surface; it can be removed with a currycomb and rub rag.

In hot weather, a shower bath can make your horse feel good. Use a garden hose, or put a little *equine* shampoo in a pail of water. Add two tablespoons of mineral oil. Start behind the ears and use a big sponge with lots of water. Rinse soap completely. Dry your horse with a sweat scraper. Bend it into a curve and, using the edge, work from the top down, following the way the hair grows. Then rub your horse down with towels and walk it until completely dry.

TACK AND
OTHER EQUIPMENT

Tack is a word horsepeople use for all the things needed to enjoy riding. It includes such items as bridle, saddle, and saddle pad, but not the grooming or stable tools, which are called stable equipment.

Buying tack is usually a one-time expense. You'll need a saddle with fittings, a *bridle* and *bit, halter* and lead shanks. Get the best saddle you can afford, styled for your particular activity. It must be comfortable, with a solid seat. Think of it as an investment. If you take good care of your investment you'll probably get your money back if you sell.

There are two styles of riding, English and Western, and many types of saddles for each style. The saddles come in all styles, sizes, and grades.

English saddles are lightweight and comfortable. They have low cantles (the upper-projecting rear part of the saddle), there is no horn, and the stirrups are made of lightweight steel. Beginning English pleasure riders should have a well-designed, straight-flapped flat saddle that fits well down behind the horse's withers, leaving enough space when the *girths* are done up to allow passage of air along its spine and no rubbing to cause a sore back. A fat horse will need a wide *tree;* a narrow, high-withered horse a narrower one.

The Western or stock type saddle is a working saddle designed for use on ranches. It has a pommel (handle) with a horn to which a lariat can be attached and often two girths. Western saddles don't buckle, but are fastened by straps which are pulled tight. The wooden or plastic stirrups are wide-bottomed for quick dismounting.

A used saddle is often a wise purchase. You save money and you don't have to break the saddle in. Be sure though that the saddle fits your horse. Most dealers will let you take a saddle home to try it.

Bridles come in different sizes and are adjustable. Your horse's bridle should fit properly. Get the same kind of bit the horse was wearing when you bought it. Never use a bit that will hurt your horse. If you don't know how, have an experienced horseperson show you the proper way to saddle your horse and adjust the bridle.

Take good care of your tack. Use Neat's-foot oil on the leather several times a year. If the stitches come out of any of your gear, take it to the saddle shop for repairs. Keep all leather clean by sponging it after use and applying a glycerine saddle soap. Hang it to dry and polish it with a soft cloth the next day. Wash your chromium-plated bit in warm water and rub it with metal polish to make it shine.

You'll need things from the hardware store: two pitchforks—one with three tines for hay and one with four or five tines for cleaning the stall—a shovel, a rake, a wheelbarrow, brooms, buckets and bucket hooks, latches, bolts, fly repellent, Neat's-foot oil, and saddle soap.

A blanket may or may not be needed, depending on your horse and where you keep it. Beginning riders should not wear spurs or carry crops. They often make matters worse and ruin the horse for riding.

9

Riding
Your
Horse

Even if your horse has been *schooled,* you must teach it to be the kind of horse you want it to be. Before you do any training, though, you must win the animal's confidence—get it to relax and trust you. Move slowly, and talk to your horse quietly. Above all, be patient. If you yell at your horse, the angry sound of your voice will be upsetting and the horse won't learn anything. Be calm and your horse will be calm. Many people believe that when they've been together for a while, a horse actually takes on its owner's temperament.

You'll learn from your horse and it will learn from you. But establish the fact right in the beginning that you are the boss. Respect your mount's size and strength, but don't be afraid of it. If you are, you've chosen the wrong horse. You must make the horse obey you immediately and completely. Don't let it get away with anything—not even once.

Continue your lessons and it will improve your riding. You'll learn to control your horse by using your weight, reins, feet, and legs. They are called *aids.* When you know how to use them correctly, your horse will respond. The more familiar you are with

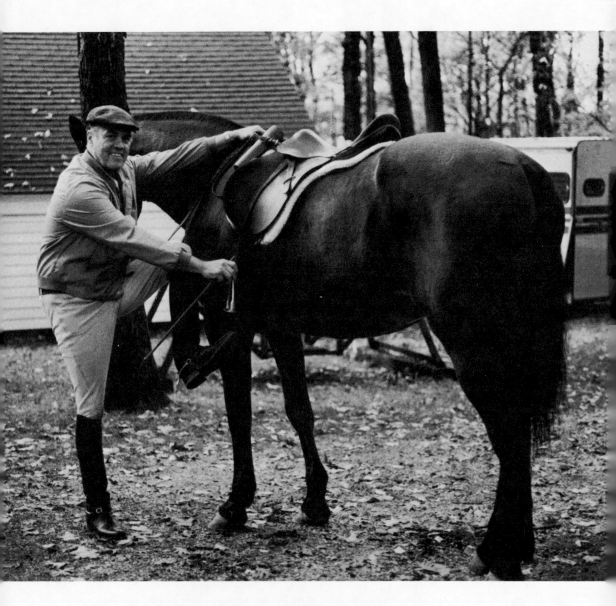

Mounting a horse

your horse and the more it gets to know you, the easier it will be. The proper use of aids will become automatic. Your horse will respond to the slightest pressure. You and your horse will be a team.

BALANCE AND TIMING

As you work with your horse, you will develop balance. When you shift and distribute your weight in time with the horse's movements, that is balance. Balance comes naturally to some people. Others have to work at it. The proper way is to sit lightly in the saddle, body erect. Distribute your weight through your thighs, knees, and feet. Your hand, or hands, should be light on the reins, giving you the feel of the horse's mouth. Relax your wrists.

With experience, timing becomes automatic. Remember, you are the boss. Your horse is waiting for your signal to tell it what to do. Do it together.

SOME DON'TS
FOR TRAIL RIDERS

Don't ride your horse directly after feeding it a full meal. Wait at least one hour.

Don't ride on city streets; the pavement can be slippery.

Don't ride along highways. Cars scare horses. Find a forest preserve bridle path, park, polo field, or farmland that is traffic-free.

Don't ride at night. Although horses see well in the dark, they are more easily frightened by noises and lights at night. Motorists can't see the horses and you are apt to cause an accident.

Don't ride near barbed wire or over rough stones.

Don't take your horse into deep water. Horses like to wade into streams, but deep water may scare and confuse them.

Don't panic if your horse bolts. Try to slow the horse down by pulling on the reins alternately with short, hard jerks. Use one rein to pull its head sideways, and get the horse going in a circle. Talk to your horse quietly to reassure and calm it.

Don't ride alone; groups are safer. Stay a horse-length behind the horse in front of you or you may get kicked.

Don't ride your horse at a fast gallop on the trail. Do a *collected* canter for a stretch, then walk your horse. You may want to do a trot for a change of pace. When you approach another horse coming in the opposite direction, always slow to a walk.

Don't bring your horse in hot and sweaty after a brisk run. A good trail rule is to walk the first mile (1.6 km) and the last mile.

Don't feed your horse grain if it is still hot from exercise. Just give it a few swallows of water or it may get stomach cramps. During cooling time, lead or ride your horse at a slow walk to avoid stiff muscles. When the horse's chest feels cool, it can eat and drink.

WINTER RIDING

If you lock your horse in the barn for the winter, you're missing a world of fun. Bundle up, saddle your horse, and get out on the trail. The horse will enjoy exercising in the clear, crisp weather. Just think of it—no flies or mosquitoes!

You needn't worry if your horse gets wet, but be sure to walk it until it's cool. Then give it a brisk rubdown. Horses, like people, can catch cold.

An unheated barn is best. If a horse is kept in a heated barn and it goes out into the cold, the sudden change in temperature can make it sick. It's not good for a horse's health, either, if it comes into a warm stall from the cold outdoors. Your horse's long hair is its protection from the cold. In most cases, it doesn't even need a winter blanket.

Some people feed their horses less in winter. A horse that works, however, should be fed the usual ration, summer or winter. Consult your vet for advice.

Many horse owners use an electric water bucket heater with a heavy rubber waterproof cord to provide the horses with water during freezing weather. Some use automatic electric waterers. A thermostatically controlled heating element heats the water.

There are riders who pull off their horse's shoes in winter. Farriers, however, caution that if you ride on trails twice a week, and walk on paved areas, your horse may fall and injure its legs if it isn't properly shod. Winter shoes also protect the horse's feet in deep snow and keep the snow from balling up. Ice-covered trails are another reason for using winter shoes.

A steel shoe with borium cleats is recommended. Borium is a type of carbide encased in a steel sheath. The farrier braises one or two borium cleats at the toe of the shoe and one at each end of the heel opening. In addition, some owners use plastic cushion pads that are inserted between the foot and the shoe. Winter shoes are more expensive than regular shoes but they may be used the following winter, depending on wear.

With the proper equipment, you and your horse can enjoy the pleasures of trail riding with friends all winter—you may even want to plan a winter picnic.

10

Keeping Your Horse Healthy

Horses are prone to sickness and lameness. Its up to you to prevent illness and injury and to keep your horse healthy and happy.

To have a healthy horse, you must work with your veterinarian. Be a good observer. Know how your horse acts and looks when it's healthy. If you think something's wrong, write down what you observed and call the veterinarian.

Keep a horse record book. In it write the dates your horse had its shots, when it was wormed, shod, and when its teeth were filed. If you change or add to its feed, write it in your book. List the dates you gave your horse first aid and tell what you did. Record expenses, too.

WAYS TO PREVENT DISEASE

Shots and vaccinations are routine in the control of disease in horses. Be sure your horse has them regularly. Your record book will tell you when it's time to call the veterinarian.

Every year, your horse should be immunized against tetanus and equine encephalomyelitis (sleeping sickness). If you show your horse, or take it to events where many horses gather, get flu shots, too. When a special problem crops up in your area, such as *strangles,* give your horse preventive shots.

Have a vet "tube worm" your horse at least twice a year to prevent sickness from internal parasites (worms). External parasites (flies, mosquitoes, ticks, lice, etc.) are also a menace and can cause disease. Administer a paste wormer to your horse every six weeks also. It can be purchased at your saddle or feed shop.

Here are some ways you can control insects:

Drain swampy areas in your vicinity.

Put up screens in the barn and keep the stalls clean.

Use insecticides in the barn and on your horse. Read labels carefully and follow directions.

There are dangerous viruses that cause equine infectious anemia (swamp fever) and there is no treatment or vaccination as yet. To find out if your horse has the virus, or is a carrier, give your animal the "Coggins Test." (In a Coggins Test, a blood sample is taken from the horse and sent to a laboratory to check for infectious equine anemia.)

EYES

Wash your horse's eyes frequently. A watery eye or tears flowing is usually a sign that the eye is irritated, probably by dust or insects. Flood the eye with clean water. Then wash it with a clean cloth dipped in boric acid solution, or as your vet recommends. Prepare the solution by dissolving two tablespoonfuls of boric acid in one cup of warm water.

TEETH

Your horse's teeth are very important for chewing and digesting its food. Irregular tooth growth may keep it from grinding food properly and may hurt the inside of its mouth. Have your horse's teeth checked at least once a year by a veterinarian. If there are any sharp points, the vet will file them down. This is called floating.

HOW TO TELL IF
YOUR HORSE IS SICK

Your horse can't tell you how it feels, but as its owner you should know the signs of good and bad health. When your horse is in good health, it will eat well, be alert, have bright eyes and a clear nose. The coat will be shiny and the dung firm.

You'll be able to tell when there is something wrong. A usually willing horse might have to be urged to move, or it may sweat more than usual. It won't eat or shows a decrease in appetite or is shivering. If you are riding your horse and you think it may be ill, bring it home immediately. Keep the animal warm and watch it carefully.

To take its temperature, put petroleum jelly on a rectal thermometer and insert it under the tail into the rectum. After three minutes, take out the thermometer and read it. A horse's normal temperature is within the range of 99 to 101°F (37–38°C). Anything above that indicates fever. Report it to the veterinarian.

If you aren't sure of how to take your horse's temperature, ask your vet to show you. Then you do it while the vet is watching. You should be able to take it yourself next time.

Another way to tell if your horse is sick is to take the pulse (expansion and contraction of the arteries) by feeling under each side of the jaw where the large artery runs. When the horse is at rest, press the artery with your middle finger gently against the inner surface of the bone. Move your index and middle finger until you can feel the pulsations. If the horse won't stand still for an entire minute, count the pulsations for fifteen seconds and multiply by four. The normal pulse rate for horses is thirty-six to forty beats per minute.

Your veterinarian can judge the seriousness of your horse's illness when you report the temperature and pulse rate.

IF YOUR HORSE IS SICK

A sick horse needs special care. Put it in the biggest stall. Be sure the bedding is clean and comfortable. Keep fresh water nearby and change it often. Allow the horse plenty of air, but keep it out of drafts. In cold weather, a blanket and leg bandages may be needed to keep the horse warm. Don't overfeed. If the horse won't eat, tempt it with apples, carrots, bran mash, and steamed oats. Add sweetened water to the hay or grain. Take away whatever it doesn't eat.

If the horse is quite ill, don't groom it. Wipe the eyes and nostrils with a soft sponge daily. Ask your vet about exercise. Lights and noises may upset it. Don't leave a sick horse alone for long. Your horse needs you around to comfort it.

YOUR FIRST AID KIT

Every horse owner should have a first aid kit and know how to use the items in it. Medical supplies aren't costly—many can be bought

SUPPLIES

Leg bandages, at least six

Gauze pads, four rolls of 2-inch (5-cm) gauze bandages, one
    package of 3-inch (8-cm) squares

Sterile absorbent cotton, one roll

Several rolls of sheet cotton

Adhesive tape, two to three 2-inch (5-cm) rolls

Vaseline

Boric acid

Epsom salts, 5-pound (2-kg) package

Blue gall remedy

Scissors

Balling gun or hypodermic syringe (22 cc)

Thermometer

Twitch

Clean pail

Sharp knife

Tweezers

Nitrofurazone antiseptic ointment

Liniment

Hydrogen peroxide (Mix ½ pint to 5 pints (237 ml to 2 l)
    of water. A good antiseptic for cleaning wounds.)

Lysol (To disinfect tools before and after use, mix 2 teaspoonfuls
    of Lysol with 1 pint (473 ml) of water. Or ask the vet to
    recommend a disinfectant.)

Glauber's salt (for constipation: one handful in feed daily)

Colic remedy (Ask vet.)

Fly repellent ointment (Ask vet.)

Antiphlogistine (for a hot poultice)

at the drugstore. On the opposite page are suggestions for the horse owner's first aid kit. Remember, though, except for minor ailments or injuries, call the veterinarian instead of trying to treat the horse yourself.

EQUINE HOSPITALS

If your horse is too ill to treat at home, is in need of surgery, or if you want an X ray and a second opinion, take your horse to a horse hospital or clinic. Many sick horses have regained their health due to the combined efforts of veterinarians, surgeons, laboratory technicians, pathologists, and others at equine hospitals.

Doctors work under well-lighted, sanitary conditions and use special equipment that can't be carried to stables. At most hospitals, twenty-four hour care is available. Patients can stay overnight or go home the day of their examination.

Besides performing surgery, veterinarians treat pneumonia, nonsurgical colic, and diseases caused by parasites. They help mares having trouble giving birth and diagnose lameness. They don't shoot horses with broken legs—most cases are handled with surgery.

Almost all human medications, with the exception of experimental drugs, are used for horses. Hospital pharmacies have penicillin, cortisone, painkillers, ointments, and antihistamines, as well as preventive medicines—vaccines, and vitamins to keep horses healthy.

The latest diagnostic tools and X-ray machines are available. X rays can be developed in less than two minutes and studied in a viewer by the veterinarian. Diagnosis is then made and treatment prescribed.

Although hospital care is costly, many horse owners feel that it's worth the money to keep their loved horses healthy.

11

Just
Think

No other animal has the special beauty, strength, and speed combined with a gentle, willing, friendly nature that the horse does. Just think of the many roles the horse has played and the jobs it has done for human beings through the years. How different our world would have been without horses!

The horse is not about to become extinct because of the invention of atomic-energy-powered machinery. Riding and caring for horses are still popular with people of all ages. The more urbanized and mechanized we become, the more we need recreation and relaxation with animals. No wonder there are so many horse lovers around.

Glossary

Aged—horse ten years old or older.

Aids—the rider's hands, back, legs, voice, and weight distribution are natural aids which control the horse. Artificial aids are the crop, spurs, and checkreins, among many others.

Appaloosa—a breed of horse with mixed colors, characterized by black or brown spots on hindquarters and loins, striped hooves, and white sclera around eyeball.

Arabian—a breed of horse that originated in Arabia.

Barb—a hardy old breed of North African desert horse.

Bay—a horse color that ranges from reddish to dark brown, horse has a black mane, tail, and points.

Bit—the metal mouthpiece of a bridle that helps control the animal.

Bloodlines—horse's ancestry (parents, grandparents, etc.).

Breed—a type of horse. Each breed is developed for a specific purpose.

Bridle—the headgear of a horse, made of leather straps with a bit that fits inside the horse's mouth, and having reins and long straps which the rider holds and uses to control the horse.

Buckskin—a tan-, beige-, or yellow-bodied horse with a black mane, tail, and legs; may have a stripe along its spine.

Canter—a smooth gait, slower than the gallop and faster than a trot.

Chestnut—reddish-brown color ranging from light red to deep copper—occasionally darker, but never black; mane and tail are of the same or a bit lighter color.

Crossbred—a horse with parents of different breeds.

Collected—on the bit with feet properly under itself; a controlled version of a natural gait such as trot or canter.

Colt—male horse or pony that is no longer nursed by its mother but under the age of four.

Conformation—the muscular and bone structure of a horse; the way a horse is put together or shaped.

Corral—a large open pen, usually with wooden rails, in which horses are kept.

Curry—to rub and clean a horse's coat with a scraper, comb, or brush.

Cutting cattle—when a rider maneuvers the horse so that a calf or cow is isolated from or "cut" from the herd. This might be done so it could be branded.

Dam—mother of a foal.

Dished face—a concave (inward-dipping) profile between the eyes and nostrils.

Draft horse—workhorse used for pulling or drawing.

Dressage—advanced training of a horse, in which a horse performs certain steps and gaits according to rider's movements and leg commands.

Equine—derived from the Latin word *equus*, or horse; of or pertaining to a horse.

Filly—a female horse or pony that is no longer nursing, but under four years of age.

Five-gaited—having the slow gait and the rack, as well as walk, trot, and canter.

Foal—horse of either sex from birth until it stops nursing.

Foundation sire—a stallion that can pass on desirable traits and is used to found a new breed. All or many horses of a certain breed can be traced to him.

Frog—the horny middle part on the bottom of a horse's foot, shaped like a triangle.

Gait—the forward movement of a horse, such as the walk, trot, canter, or gallop. The sequence in which one foot follows another determines the gait.

Gelding—a male horse that has been neutered by surgery. His testes (organs that produce sperm and male hormones) have been removed and he can no longer be used for breeding.

Girth—the band or strap that encircles the body of a horse and holds the saddle in place.

Grade horse—a horse or pony that is not of any special breed.

Green horse—a horse that has very little or no training.

Groom—someone who cleans and takes care of stabling needs of horses; or to clean and brush a horse.

Halfbred—a horse with one purebred parent.

Halter—a rope or leather headpiece put around a horse's head to which a rope or chain may be attached for leading or tying up the horse.

Hand—a unit of measure used to determine a horse's height from the ground to the withers; one hand equals 4 inches (10 cm).

Lead shank—a rope or line attached to the horse's halter in order to lead the horse.

Light horse—any horse used for riding or driving that is not a draft breed.

Lipizzaners—an all-white breed of horse that originated in Austria, trained to give dressage exhibitions.

Mare—a mature female horse or pony.

Morgan—a small, powerful breed of horse; the foundation sire and owner both named Justin Morgan.

Mount—a horse you ride; or to get on a horse.

Mustang—naturalized horse of the West, descended from horses brought to New World by Spanish.

Paddock—a small field or fenced-in area for horses near the barn.

Paint or pinto—a horse with white or colored spots or irregular markings on its coat.

Palomino—a golden or light-brown horse with a white or cream mane and tail.

Pedigree—a list of the horse's ancestors.

Points—certain parts of a horse of special importance in judging its strength and soundness.

Pony—a full-grown equine animal not more than 14.2 hands.

Purebred—a horse whose sire and dam belong to the same breed, and that is accepted in the official registry of its breed.

Quarter Horse—a sturdy breed of horse known for its speed up to a quarter of a mile (.4 km).

Rack—a fast, flashy four-beat gait, all four of the horse's feet hitting the ground separately.

Registered—a pure-blooded horse receives a paper called its pedigree when its owner registers it with the headquarters of the particular breed.

Schooling—training a horse.

Shying—a sudden sideways movement of a horse caused by fright.

Sire—father of a horse or pony.

Stallion—a full-grown male horse able to become a father.

Standardbred—a breed of racehorse that pulls two-wheeled sulkies on the racetrack.

Stockings—white leg markings on a horse.

Strangles—highly contagious bacterial disease of the nose and throat.

Tack—equipment such as the saddle, harness, bridle, and bit.

Thoroughbred—a breed of racehorse developed by crossing Arabian stallions with English mares.

Tree—the wooden structure under the leather of the saddle—the framework.

Trot—the natural gait of a horse that is between a walk and a canter; the front and hind feet on opposite sides move together.

Wean—take a young horse from its mother and feed it something other than mother's milk.

Withers—the top of a horse's shoulders; they make a small hump at the base of a horse's neck just behind its front legs.

Yearling—a colt or filly between one and two years of age.

English saddle, 67
English Shire, 32, 34
Eohippus, 3–4, 44
Equine, 82
Equine Hospitals, 79
Equus, 4, 7
Expenses, 49–50

Feathers, 32
Feeding, 59, 61
Filly, 12, 82
First aid kit, 77–79
Five-gaited, 24, 83
Fjording, 48
Flashy rack, 24
Foal, 5–6, 12–14, 41, 82–83
Foundation sire, 22, 27, 83
Four-beat lateral gait, 38
Frog, 66, 83

Gait, 10–11, 20, 23–24, 27, 38, 83
Gallop, 10–11
Gelding, 1, 13, 55, 83
Grade horse, 50–52, 83
Great Horse, 6
Green Horse, 54–55, 83
Grooming, 62, 65–66

Hackney Pony, 48
Haflinger, 48
Half-Arabian, 20
Halfbred, 19, 83
Halter, 83
Hand, 9, 83
Health, 74–77
Hearing, 9
Height, 9
Highland Pony, 48

Horsemanship, 49
Horse registry, 26

Instincts, 8
Intelligence, 8, 39
International Arabian Horse Association, 20
Irish ponies, 46–48

Jennets, 21, 38
Jumping, 20, 24, 36

Kentucky Derby, 22

Lead shank, 83
Light horse, 83
Lipizzaner, 39, 41–42, 83
Lope, 39

Mares, 13, 55, 84
Memory, 8
Mesohippus, 4
Merychippus, 4
Mestenos, 21
Miniatures, 39, 44
Misty of Chincoteague, 45
Morgan, 23–24, 27, 84
Mount, 84
Mustangs, 21–22, 31, 84

Naragansett Pacers, 24
Nez Perce, 35
Norfolk Trotters, 26
Norwegian Fjord Pony, 48

Pace, 11, 26
Paddock, 58, 84
Paint, 12, 36, 84
Paints, 11, 84
Palominos, 12, 20, 34–36, 51, 84